RETURN OF THE GREAT GODDESS

RETURN OF THE
GREAT GODDESS

edited by
BURLEIGH MUTÉN

STEWART, TABORI & CHANG
New York

Published in 1997 and distributed by
Stewart, Tabori & Chang,
a division of U.S. Media Holdings, Inc.
575 Broadway, New York, NY 10012

Distributed in Canada by
General Publishing Company Ltd.
30 Lesmill Road
Don Mills, Ontario, M3B 2T6, Canada

Distributed in all other territories by
Grantham Book Services Ltd.
Isaac Newton Way, Alma Park Industrial Estate
Grantham, Lincs NG31 9SD, England

Library of Congress Cataloging-in-Publication Data

Return of the great goddess / edited by Burleigh Mutén
        p. cm.
  Originally published: Boston : Shambhala ; [New York?] :
  Distributed in the U.S. by Random House, 1994.
      ISBN 1-55670-608-1 (pbk.)
      1. Goddesses.   2. Goddess religion.   I. Mutén, Burleigh.
  [BL325.F4R48 1997]
  291.2'114—dc21   97-5529

Printed in Singapore

10 9 8 7 6 5 4 3 2 1

First STC paperback edition

To my mother
Winifred Jones Newmann
daughter of
Burley Brant Jones
daughter of
Cornelia Rackmyer Brant

and to my daughter
Iris Dagmar Mutén

CONTENTS

INTRODUCTION

You must give birth to your images.
They are the future waiting to be born.
—RAINER MARIA RILKE

After a five-thousand-year reign of male icons in the Western world, we have the exhilarating privilege of witnessing a global reappearance of the Divine Feminine in the arts and in religious ceremony. Women's history suddenly reveals a legacy of authority, leadership, and wisdom, dating back some thirty thousand years, inspiring a new integrity in the women of this century and in our daughters and sons and their daughters and sons to come.

There was a time on Earth when the cycles of a woman's body, her blood, birthing, and mothering experiences were celebrated and honored. There was a time on Earth when her sexuality and intuition were considered holy. The word *virgin* had nothing to do with celibacy; it was about independence. There was a time on Earth when women were considered the sacred daughters of Gaia, the ground of our being. For over two thousand years *the* religious experience in classical Greece was the annual initiation at Eleusis, a religion centered on the mother and daughter, Demeter and Persephone.

During the past twenty years, women have been making pilgrimages to Delphi and to Crete, to Ireland and Anatolia, where matristic cultures thrived some twenty to thirty thousand years ago. In sacred caves and on the sites of temples dedicated to Gaia and to Hestia and Brigit, women from all over the globe are rituraling to sing praise of Earth, our Mother, and to pray for Her healing. A global community of women walk together, validating the experiences and ethics that we share as women.

Overlooking the vast valley at Delphi, a circle of fifty women in the olive grove sacred to Athena raise their voices to the sky, singing, "You can't kill the spirit; it is old and strong. Like a mountain She goes on and on." In a field of ferns rosy with dusk, four women join hands and call to Nemesis, Tara, White Buffalo Calf Woman, and Hera to guide them as they sit in the sacred space they've created on the forest floor. After tucking her children into bed, a woman, alone, lights a candle, placing a small statue of Isis alongside the toy of her ill child as she asks Isis, the healing mother, to bless him with health.

On the altar cloth in the center of women's circles all over the United States and Europe, New Zealand, and Australia, women place figurines of Inanna and Lilith, Sheila-na-gig, the Birthing Goddess of Old Anatolia, Artemis, Tara, Kuan-yin, and Kali. Symbols from the prehistoric era have become familiar within the women's community on Earth again.

The ancient images inform us of the courage and mystery of carrying, birthing, and nourishing a child from our own breasts. The ancient images remind us of the integrity of bleeding without injury, and of our own blood's relationship to the moon and the sea tides. They stir something deep within the psyche that shows up in our dreams as old women who guide and protect, as owls and snakes and dogs, the goddesses' companions. The ancient symbols re-call our feminine heritage as we re-create community among women unlike anything our mothers knew. Together we affirm our innate goodness, free of shame and fear.

In the Hindu tradition, an image of the Divine is not considered a symbol or an idol; it is the real thing. In the practice of *darshan*, viewing the statue of a particular deity is equivalent to being in the presence of that deity. As the devotee beholds the Divine, the Divine in turn beholds the devotee and bestows a blessing.

In the spirit of *darshan*, I offer this anthology for your reflection. All of the images and literary passages have been selected to remind you of your own natural majesty as newborn, little girl, young woman, leader, lady of the beasts and plants, seer, spirit-bearer, life-giver, protectress, dancer, priestess, magician, athlete, musician, politician, elder, visionary, poet, pathfinder, death-wielder, teacher, healer, adventuress, explorer, inventor, sister, friend, daughter, lover, huntress, ritual-maker, crone, goddess, oldest of the old.

BURLEIGH MUTÉN
February 2, 1994

RETURN OF THE GREAT GODDESS

We never know how high we are
Till we are asked to rise
And then if we are true to plan
Our statures touch the skies—

EMILY DICKINSON

The Goddess is first of all earth, the dark, nurturing mother who brings forth all life. She is the power of fertility and generation; the womb, and also the receptive tomb, the power of death. All proceeds from Her; all returns to Her. As earth, She is also plant life; trees, the herbs and grains that sustain life. She is the body, and the body is sacred.

STARHAWK
The Spiral Dance

Roberta Baskin Shefrin, *Woman,* 1985

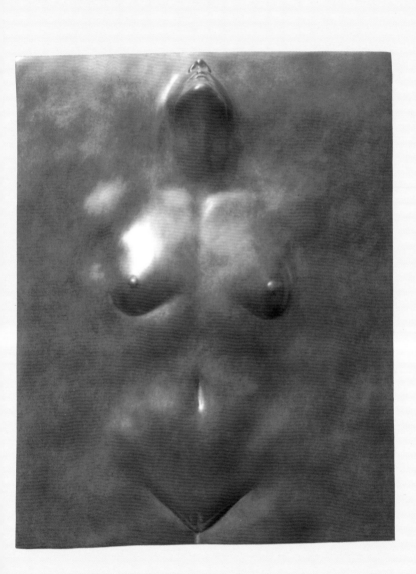

THOU GAIA ART I

the earth quivers, wherever I go
in these zones of ripeness,
and sends out gentle visible waves—

through all things it vibrates in me,
wherever I happen to be
on the drifting floes—

you are the riddle under my feet
the depths in me, wherever I am
you are everywhere—

for Thou Gaia Art I

HEIDE GÖTTNER-ABENDROTH

Christopher Gowell, *I'm My Own Guardian Angel,* 1993

All Nature . . . . dies and is born again

Seeds . . . . die and are born again

Plants . . . . die and are born again

The years . . . . die and are born again

The moon, the sun . . . . die and are born again

We . . . . die and are born again

Mother-Daughter
Mother-Daughter
Mother-Daughter

DONNA WILSHIRE
Virgin Mother Crone

Jim Schlessinger, *Burd and Abby, 1983*

In the start of time, splendor appeared. . . . It was the Mother. She was all that was. She divided the sky from the sea and danced upon the waves. A wind gathered behind Her from Her swift dancing. When She rubbed this wind between Her hands, it became the Great Serpent. She took him to Her and loved him, and a great egg grew within Her and She became a Dove. The Dove-Mother brooded over the egg until it was ready. Then out of the egg came all things—sun, moon, stars, earth, mountains, rivers, and all living creatures. The splendor of the Mother flowed through everything, through sun and sea, through the veins of the earth into root and leaf, into grain and fruit, into all women and men. And each birth became forever an acceptance of splendor and each death a gift to the Great Mother.

JUNE RACHUY BRINDEL
Ariadne

Imogen Cunningham, *Martha Graham 2, 1931*

We say the time of waiting is over.
We say the silence has been broken.
We say there can be no forgetting now.
We say
              listen

We are the bones
of your grandmother's grandmothers.
We have returned now
We say you cannot forget us now
We say we are with you
And you are us.

PATRICIA REIS
from "The Ancient Ones"

I who am the beauty of the green earth and the white moon among the stars and the mysteries of the waters, I call upon your soul to arise and come unto me. For I am the soul of nature that gives life to the universe. From Me all things proceed and unto me they must return. Let My worship be in the heart that rejoices, for behold— all acts of love and pleasure are My rituals. Let there be beauty and strength, power and compassion, honor and humility, mirth and reverence within you. And you who seek to know Me, know that your seeking and yearning will avail you not, unless you know the Mystery: for if that which you seek, you find not within yourself, you will never find it without. For behold, I have been with you from the beginning, and I am that which is attained at the end of desire.

DOREEN VALIENTE/STARHAWK ADAPTATION
"The Charge of the Goddess"

Evelyn de Buhr, left panel from *Bathers Triptych,* 1990

Epiphany

Lynn Schmidt says
>she saw You once as prairie grass,
>Nebraska prairie grass,

>she climbed out of her car on a hot highway
>leaned her butt on the nose of her car,
>looked out over one great flowing field,
>stretching beyond her sight until the horizon came:
>*vastness,* she says,
>responsive to the *slightest shift* of wind,
>>full of infinite change,
>>all One.

>She says when she can't pray
>She calls up Prairie Grass.

PEM KREMER

Kendrick Anne Wronski, *Planting the Seeds,* 1992

She is the egg and the seed of the world. . . . She is darkness as well as light. Her cycles encompass all moods and all phases. She is queen of the Bright Night and of the Darkness, guide to the lost traveller and pathway to the underworld. She brings creativity and visions; she also brings sleep, darkness and death. . . . She is the home of the souls of the unborn and of the dead waiting for re-birth.

ANNE KENT RUSH
Moon, Moon

Suzanne Benton, *The Seer,* 1987

Women, please let your own sun, your
concentrated energy, your own submerged
authentic vital power shine out from you.

We are no longer the moon.
Today we are truly the sun.
We will build shining golden cathedrals
at the top of crystal mountains, East of
the Land of the Rising Sun.

Women, when you paint your own portrait,
do not forget to put the golden dome at
the top of your head.

RAICHO HIRATSUKO
from "Women's Manifesto" (1911)
translated by Mayumi Oda

White Tara, 17th-century Tibet

Our Mother who art in Earth and Heaven,
(as we are in the MOTHER
and HEAVEN is in us)
Hallowed, respectful, joyful thy name.
Thy holy realm is already come.
Thy will awaits us to be done.
Give us this day the strength to love,
To be the lion and the dove.
Forgive us as we tread your flowers,
Ignoring duties that are ours.
Lead us from annihilation
TO CELEBRATE ALL CREATION,
For we share in the life and in the power
And in the glory forever and ever.

PRISCILLA BAIRD HINCKLEY
The New Our Father

Bobbi Carrey, *Terra Firma, 1974*

Water (woman) that is the essense of you.
He na tye (woman) that is recognition and remembering.
Gentle. Soft. Sure.
Long shadows of afternoon, growing as the light turns
west toward sleep. Turning with the sun.
(The rest of it is continents and millennia.
(How could I have waited so long for completion?)

The water rises around us like the goddess coming home.
(Arisen.) Same trip, all things considered, all times
and visions, all places and spaces taken into account
on that ancient journey, finally returned. The maps, the plans,
the timetables: the carefully guided tours into all manner
of futilities. Manners the last turn in the road: arid irony.

(Lady, why does your love so touch me?
(Lady, why do my hands have strength for you?
(Lady, how could I wander so long without you?

PAULA GUNN ALLEN
from "He Na Tye Woman"

Rodger Kingston, *Cia with Stars*, Albuquerque, NM 1993

Wisdom calls aloud in the streets,
She raises Her voice in the public squares;
She calls out at the street corners,
She delivers Her message at the city gates.

Proverbs 1:20–21

Carol Sevick, *She Speaks for Peace,* 1991

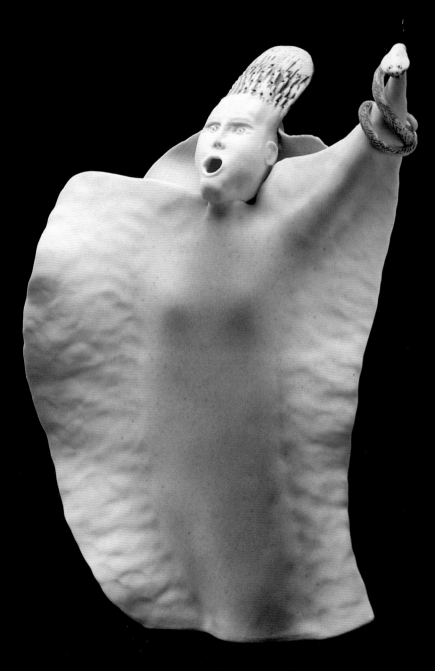

WE NEED A GOD WHO BLEEDS NOW

we need a god who bleeds now
a god whose wounds are not
some small male vengeance
some pitiful concession to
      humility
a desert swept with dryin
      marrow in honor of the
      lord

we need a god who bleeds
spreads her lunar vulva &
      showers us in shades
      of scarlet
thick & warm
      like the breath of her
our mothers tearing
      to let us   in
this place breaks open
like our mothers bleeding

the planet is heaving
      mourning our ignorance
the moon tugs the seas
to hold her / to hold her
embrace swelling hills / i am
not wounded i am bleeding
      to life

we need a god who bleeds now
whose wounds are not
      the end of anything

NTOZAKE SHANGE

Mark Weiss, *Mother Earth*, 1990

As it was in the beginning,
  I say:
  Here is your sacrament—

    Take. Eat. This is my body,
    this real milk, thin, sweet, bluish,
    which I give for the life of the world.
    Like sap to spring it rises
    even before the first faint cry is heard,
    an honest nourishment
    alone able to sustain you.

ROBIN MORGAN
from "The Network of the Imaginary Mother"

Martina Hoffmann, *Birthscape II,* 1988

The valley spirit never dies;
It is the woman, primal mother.
Her gateway is the root of heaven and earth.
It is like a veil barely seen.
Use it; it will never fail.

Tao Te Ching Verse Six
translated by Gia-Fu Feng *and* Jane English

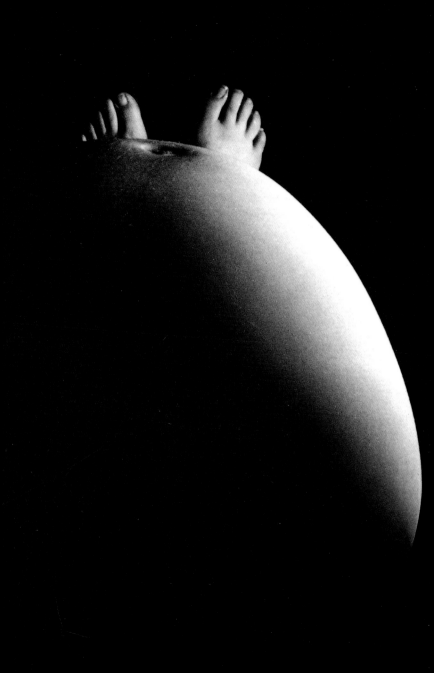

When the first man entered a cave and witnessed the first woman's magic of drawing forth a new person from her body, Themis was there. "The young shall be fed and nurtured, protected and loved." The humans increased in number, living together in small groups. They shared meat, nuts, plants, shelter, and the pleasure of their bodies. Themis was with them. "All who shared the bond of a woman's womb, you are her Family. You are indivisible." The families multiplied, each woman giving birth within the aura of her mother's protection. Themis saw their needs. "All the families descended from one womb are a clan. Stay together. Listen to the elders as I guide them."

. . . In this way, millennia passed and Greece prospered in her infancy. Innocence ended abruptly. Barbarian invaders swept down through her mainland and later her islands. They seized Themis at the outset. With the Goddess a bound captive, the invaders proclaimed the new order: Children must be named after their fathers; cities must be fortified; power must be worshipped. They established their new god, Zeus, who ruled by the terror of his thunderbolt and procreated by deception and rape. Yet Themis would not be silenced. "You dare not crush the primal Order. When your new gods and your mutilations of our old Goddesses assemble on Mount Olympus, I alone will have the right to convoke them. I will not die."

CHARLENE SPRETNAK
The Myth of Themis
from *Lost Goddesses of Early Greece*

Yosemite, circa 1900

I am daughter, sister, mother in thousands of generations of women, women whose skills created peaceful and bountiful civilizations, women who preserved remnants of our knowledge when the civilizations passed.

I am a woman. In me lives the knowledge and experience of all beings. I can use that knowledge and experience to create a loving, spontaneous world. . . .

I am a woman, a part of and the whole of the first circle, the circle that transcends space and time, the circle of women joined.

I am a woman, a human being of extraordinary strength, wisdom and grace.

And this is true.

ANN VALLIANT and
THE WOMANCRAFT GUIDE MANUAL COLLECTIVE
from "I am a woman"

Belle Johnson, *Three Women with Long Hair,* circa 1900

If you focus enough on the Goddess, it is almost as if she begins to notice you and takes you under her wing. She gradually begins to reveal herself in all her complexity, and sometimes in unexpected ways. This is an ongoing process, spiralling to deeper and deeper levels, always continuing.

. . . Let the Goddesses come into your meditations, your dreams, your work and the faces of people around you. You will begin to recognize and acknowledge the Goddess in your life and become fertile soil for her to grow in. Give her plenty of water, light and food, and you will find yourself transformed by what grows inside you. You will have become the Goddess.

HALLIE IGLEHART AUSTEN
The Heart of the Goddess

Glenn Ruga, from *El Proyecto Holyoke / The Holyoke Project,* 1989

Her shrines were found everywhere, for everywhere is her abode—near the hearth, at the sacred well or spring that provides water for drink and healing, in the ancient grove of trees forming Nature's cathedral, in the deepest cave, on the highest mountain. The plants and animals, the moon, sun and stars, the river that flows to the sea and the ocean itself: all were her domain. All were sacred to the Goddess. All were recognized as forming part of the Great Mother and therefore as kin.

ADELE GETTY
Goddess

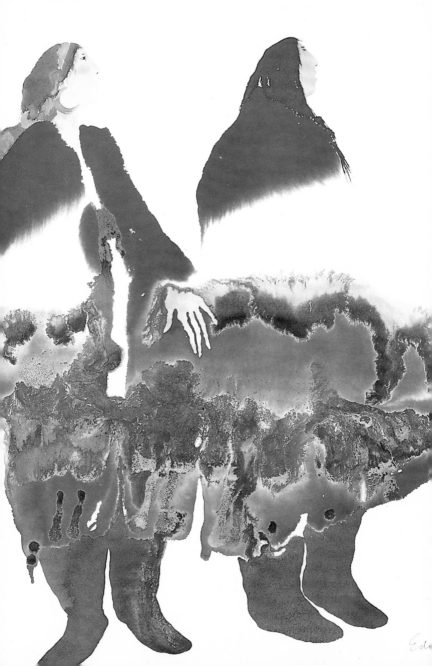

Intuition is the treasure of a woman's psyche. It is like a divining instrument and like a crystal through which one can see with uncanny interior vision. It is like a wise old woman who is with you always, who tells you *exactly what the matter is, tells you exactly whether you need to go left or right.* It is a form of The One Who Knows, old La Que Sabé, the Wild Woman.

. . .

Ask within for her advice.
She is the Mother of the Ages.
Nothing surprises her.
She has seen it all.

CLARISSA PINKOLA ESTÉS
Women Who Run with the Wolves

Nona Hatay, *Fräulein Berta Himmler,* 1967

For this moment we will
    remember the fire
as our sacred flame in
    the wells of the temples.
We will remember the
    dark blue and white mosaic
patterns that swirled
    as we danced.
We will remember the women
    hand in hand,
    moving to the
blue flame that emerged from
    the darkness of the earth.

And the cicada tells us
    it is time.

For this moment our serpents
    uncoil together.
Deep into my spiral
    I weave into yours,

and within the beat,
    my body sways,
    touching yours.
Old One, Wise One,
our palms press
our hearts breathe
our spirits dance our power,
    knowing the sacred flame
lives.
It is ours inside forever!
Together, we dance the return.
We shapeshift our place,
    our time.
For one moment across the sands
I become you and you become
    me
    The Old Ones
    The Wise Ones
    The Ancient Ones.

ECLIPSE
from "Cicada"

George Segal, *The Dancers* (1971), © 1997 by George Segal/Licensed by VAGA, New York.

Thank you, my dear

You came, and you did
well to come: I needed
you. You have made

love blaze up in
my breast—bless you!
Bless you as often

as the hours have
been endless to me
while you were gone

SAPPHO
verse 46
translated by Mary Barnard

Judy Chicago, *Sappho* plate from *The Dinner Party,* 1979

It was in Crete that the snake aspect of the Mother Goddess religion reached its highest development, and there the beautiful remains of a great civilization have been unearthed. The snake in Cretan society represented the wisdom of the goddess and was associated with life, death, and regeneration. Venerated as a protector of the household, the snake was also considered the reincarnation of a dead family member. Special rooms equipped with snake tubes (which enabled snakes to travel through the house) were found in many homes.

JUDY CHICAGO
The Dinner Party

Irene Young, *Snake Goddess at Knossos,* 1989

HYMN TO SELENE

Sing, Muses, of the moon
    with long wings
from whose divine head
    sky-revealed lustre
spirals down to earth and great
adornment arises from her
    gleaming
radiance. The unillumined air
    glitters
from her golden
    crown—beams are
released in the sky whenever
on the evening of
    the full moon
far-shining Selene bathes
    her soft
skin in Ocean and clothes
    herself,
and yoking her foals, radiant,
    proud,

she drives the beautiful-maned
    horses
eagerly before her,
    so completing a
great cycle—rays come
    brightest
from the sky when she waxes.
A sure sign for mortals is this:
She conceived and begot
    a daughter
Pandeia, Enchantress, magician,
pre-eminent beauty among
    immortals.
Hail Selene, white-armed Queen
of the sky with flowing hair.

Homeric Hymn 32
translated by Ronald Basto

Joan Bredin-Price, *Drawing Down the Moon,* 1992

The spiritual world is like the natural world—only diversity will save it. Just as the health of a forest or fragrant meadow can be measured by the number of different insects and plants and creatures that successfully make it their home, so only by an extraordinary abundance of disparate spiritual and philosophic paths will human beings navigate a pathway through the dark and swirling storms that mark our current era. "Not by one avenue alone," wrote Symmachus sixteen centuries ago, "can we arrive at so tremendous a secret."

MARGOT ADLER
Drawing Down the Moon

Carl Larsson, detail of *Model Writing Picture Postals,* 1906

In the beginning, people prayed to the Creatress of Life, the Mistress of Heaven. At the very dawn of religion, God was a woman. Do you remember?

MERLIN STONE
When God Was a Woman

Carol Keiser, *Virgin de La Salud,* 1991

QUEEN MEDUSA

Here I sing of the Muses
    who gift the earth
    with vision and voice
    and of their cousin,

    Fair Medusa
of the shining gold wings.

Hallowed healer whose
wisdom has been hidden
lo! these eons, turn now,
show the crown of
deathchange and rebirth
that sits upon your
    serpent hair.
    Show the strong beauty
    that has always been
    yours,
    Queen of the Deep Sea,
    Queen of the deep,
      red blood.

Low on the horizon
the dark moon widens
    to a crescent smile.
      Mother of Pegasus,
      I welcome you.

BURLEIGH MUTÉN

Audrey Flack, *Colossal Head of Medusa,* 1991

The mother of us all,
the oldest of all,
hard,
     splendid as rock

Whatever there is that is of the land
      it is she
          who nourishes it,
      it is the Earth
          that I sing.

HOMER
"Hymn to the Earth"
translated by Charles Boer

Retha Gambaro, *Daughter of Mother Earth,* 1991

The Delphic Oracle, who was the High-priestess of the ancient world, has been silent for fifteen hundred years now. Nobody in the ancient world wrote a history of this priesthood, although many knew some of her personal names. Her title was Pythia, Dragon Priestess of Earth.

Many writers recorded some of her oracles, which were her words. All knew her first motto: "Know thyself."

NORMA LORRE GOODRICH
Priestesses

Leonard Baskin, *Sybil with Crow,* 1991

Over the last one hundred years, some one thousand engravings, reliefs, and sculptures of female images have been found, dating from ca. 30,000–9000 BC. Such figurines are found across a vast area of Europe, from Siberia and the Ukraine to Germany, France, and Italy. This means that for more than twenty thousand years, a Great Goddess existed in our mythic and religious imagination, art, rituals, and lives. What these images tell us is that in earliest periods of human consciousness, the creative impulse was imagined as female.

. . . In coal, bone, and stone, her body is sculpted with great egg shapes—breast, belly, and buttocks—images of fullness and potential becoming.

PATRICIA REIS
Through the Goddess: A Woman's Way of Healing

Gabriele Johannsmann, *Sheer Lust,* 1991

I see the wise woman.

She carries a blanket of compassion. She wears a robe of wisdom. Around her throat flutters a veil of shifting shapes. From her shoulders, a mantle of power flows. A story band encircles her forehead. She stitches a quilt; she spins fibers into yarn; she knits; she sews; she weaves. She ties the threads of our lives together. She forms a web of spiraling threads.

SUSUN WEED
Healing Wise

Frank Ward, *Carmen Santiago,* 1990

THE INVOCATION TO KALI

It is time for the invocation:

Kali, be with us.
Violence, destruction,
        receive our homage.
Help us to bring darkness
        into the light,
To lift out the pain, the anger,
Where it can be seen
        for what it is—
The balance-wheel for our
        vulnerable, aching love.
Put the wild hunger where it
        belongs,
Within the act of creation,
Crude power that forges
        a balance
Between hate and love.

Help us to be the
        always hopeful
Gardeners of the spirit
Who know that without
        darkness
Nothing comes to birth
As without light
Nothing flowers.

Bear the roots in mind,
You, the dark one, Kali,
Awesome power.

MAY SARTON

Sudha Mookerjee, *Goddess Kali,* 1954

The Second Coming

Clouds out of darkness,
Pillow white, they float,
As dawn slides open.
Slowly, the kinswoman
Parachutes gentle free
Arriving with gravity,
Cleaving, to earth,
As Seagull does to nest.

Oracle of all dreams,
Chalice, shelter, wing,
Harvesting molten treasure,
Flowing through sun gold
Feathers and life air
    of Anatolia.

Ancient fire haired druid,
    mariner,
Tiamat, Diana, moon world
    goddess,

Eating the ripe sea,
    the sensuous air,
Gleaning and swelling
    the life source
Into a vivid, retina burning,
    sun flood.
Drenching all completeness
    with desire
To search sweet for
    inner seed,
Kindling, bringing to light
    what is
Herself, the kinswoman.

SUZANNE BENTON

Mayumi Oda, *Goddess Hears People's Needs and Comes*, 1976

A Pledge of Allegiance to the Family of Earth

I pledge allegiance to the Earth,
and to the flora, fauna
and human life that it supports,
one planet, indivisible,
with safe air, water and soil,
economic justice, equal rights
and peace for all.

Women's Environment and
Development Organization
of the Women's Foreign
Policy Council

Mark Meunier, *Statue of Liberty,* 1986

There was a time when you were not a slave, remember that. You walked alone, full of laughter, you bathed bare-bellied. You say you have lost all recollection of it, remember. You know how to avoid meeting a bear on the track. You know the winter fear when you hear the wolves gathering. But you can remain seated for hours in the tree-tops to await morning. You say there are no words to describe this time, you say it does not exist. But remember. Make an effort to remember. Or, failing that, invent.

MONIQUE WITTIG
Les Guérillères

TO MY LAST PERIOD

well girl, goodbye,
after thirty-eight years.
thirty-eight years and you
never arrived
splendid in your red dress
without trouble for me
somewhere, somehow.

now it is done,
and I feel just like
the grandmothers who,
after the hussy has gone,
sit holding her photograph
and sighing, *wasn't she
beautiful? wasn't she beautiful?*

LUCILLE CLIFTON

Richard Yarde, *Josephine Baker Baffle,* center panel of triptych, 1992–1993

They summoned forth the Night
and the Deities of the Night
from the nether world, praying to Hecate
in plaintive, howling cries:
"You, Trivia, potent goddess
of the triple crossroad, come,
You who know all our plans,
aiding and abetting our incantations
and the arts of the Magician."

OVID
compiled from *Metamorphoses*
14.404–5 and 7.194–95
translated by Ronald Basto

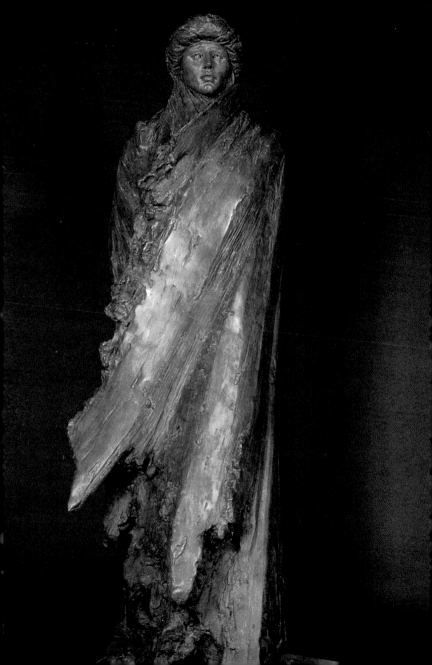

The return to the Goddess is not focussed on transcendence, but on the embodiment of the sacred, in life and in relationships. The unification of the body, sexuality and emotions with the spirit, the return from striving to being. . . .

As part of my awareness of the Goddess, I have reclaimed the altar. In ancient times, for example in Minoan civilization, there was an altar in every room of the home. The home was where spirit lived. . . .

My altars are the stage for my soul. They change as I do. If I am calling forth some part of myself in my life, for example Eros, I place on my altar something that represents that to me, a postcard of Aphrodite. Thus there is a dynamic between the outer and inner life.

TSULTRIM ALLIONE
from "Sky Dancer"

Gaston Lachaise, *Garden Figure*, circa 1935

Butterfly Maiden is the female fertilizing force. Carrying the pollen from one place to another, she cross-fertilizes, just as the soul fertilizes mind with night-dreams, just as archetypes fertilize the mundane world. She is the center. She brings the opposites together by taking a little from here and putting it there. Transformation is no more complicated than that. This is what she teaches. This is how the butterfly does it. This is how the soul does it.

CLARISSA PINKOLA ESTÉS
Women Who Run with the Wolves

Michael Kuch, *The Night Stitcher*, 1991

POEM IN PRAISE OF MENSTRUATION

if there is a river
more beautiful than this
bright as the blood
red edge of the moon   if

there is a river
more faithful than this
returning each month
to the same delta   if there

is a river
braver than this
coming and coming in a surge
of passion, of pain   if there
    is

a river
more ancient than this
daughter of eve
mother of cain and
    abel   if there is in

the universe such a river   if
there is some where water
more powerful than this wild
water
pray that it flows also
through animals
beautiful and faithful
    and ancient
and female and brave

LUCILLE CLIFTON

Leah Korican, *Totem,* 1992

Huge muscles
     hump over my shoulders
The tendons of my thighs
     flex in and out
My neck turns
     toward the stars
Water laps around my ankles
     I become
     The Power
     Of the Universe.

JOANNE LANICOTTI
from *The Birth Project*

Judy Chicago, *The Crowning,* 1984

Goddess of wire spark
Goddess of gold
Goddess of glow
Goddess below above
DOWNTOWN
UPTOWN
ALL AROUND GODDESS
Goddess of on time
Goddess of too late
Goddess of wait
WAIT WAIT WAIT
walk
Goddess of high HEEL
GODDESS OF TRUCK ROAR
GODDESS OF SIRENS
GODDESS OF EDGES
GODDESS OF
    ORANGE DIVIDER
      CONES

GODDESS OF
    FLOWER STANDS
GODDESS OF
    CIGARETTE BUTTS
GODDESS OF WASTE PAPER
GODDESS OF WASTE
GODDESS OF PAPER
GODDESS OF WASTE
GODDESS OF GREEN EXIT
GODDESS OF
    WHITE ENTER
GOING GODDESS
GODDESS RETURNING
GODDESS GOING
RETURNING GODDESS
GODDESS WHO
    NEVER LEFT

LEAH KORICAN
from "City Goddess"

Jane Bregoli, *Crepuscule in Black and Brown: Wendy,* 1992

RE-MEMBER US

Re-member us,
you who are living,
restore us, renew us.
Speak for our silence.
Continue our work.
Bless the breath of life.
Sing of the hidden patterns.
Weave the web of peace.

JUDITH ANDERSON

Judith Anderson, *Re-member Us,* 1990

There was a time when there was no distinction among this Primordial Goddess, the Earth, and Earth's daughter, Woman. All were one, part of the mysterious female universe. The human race, awed by this nameless force, watched plants grow from the body of the Earth and life spring from the body of Woman, and could only venerate this magical power possessed by the feminine spirit.

JUDY CHICAGO
The Dinner Party

Sarah Chester McKusick, *Unfolding Earth,* 1995.

How might your life have been different if there had been a place for you . . . a place of women, where you were received and affirmed? A place where other women, perhaps somewhat older, had been affirmed before you, each in her time, affirmed, as she struggled to become more truly herself.

A place where, after the fires were lighted, and the drumming, and the silence, there would be a hush of expectancy filling the entire chamber . . . a knowing that each woman there was leaving old conformity to find her self . . . a sense that all of womanhood stood on a threshold.

And if, during the hush, the other women, slightly older, had helped you to trust your own becoming . . . to trust it and quietly and prayerfully to nurture it.

How might your life be different?

JUDITH DUERK
Circle of Stones

Elizabeth Catlett, *Three Women of America,* 1990

WHEN A WOMAN FEELS ALONE

"When a woman feels alone, when the room
Is full of daemons," the Nootka tribe
Tells us, "The Old Woman will be there."
She has come to me over three thousand miles
And what does she have to tell me, troubled
"by phantoms in the night"?
Is she really here?
What is the saving word from so deep in the past,
From as deep as the ancient root of the redwood,
From as deep as the primal bed of the ocean,
From as deep as a woman's heart sprung open
Again through a hard birth or a hard death?
Here under the shock of love, I am open
To you, Primal Spirit, one with rock and wave,
One with the survivors of flood and fire,
Who have rebuilt their homes a million times,
Who have lost their children and borne them again.
The words I hear are strength, laughter, endurance.
Old Woman I meet you deep inside myself.
There in the rootbed of fertility,
World without end, as the legend tells it.
Under the words you are my silence.

MAY SARTON

Deidre Scherer, *After Light,* 1990

Wherever you go, I will go.
Wherever you lodge, I will lodge.
Your people shall be my people.
Where you die, I will die;
and there I will be buried.

The Book of Ruth
1:16−17

For forty weeks, day and night, Noah and Namah's children floated in the waters of her womb. When her waters finally broke, all the creatures of the earth burst forth and fed from her breasts until she became dry.

DEBORAH KRUGER
"Namah's Womb: A Woman's Midrash of Noah's Ark"

FOR 40 WEEKS DAY AND NIGHT NOAH & NAMAH'S CHILDREN FLOATED IN THE WATERS FINALLY BROKE ALL THE CREATURES WOMB WHEN HER WATERS OF THE EARTH BURST FORTH AND FED FROM HER BREASTS UNTIL SHE BECAME DRY

I get started early, before six. It promises to be a good laundry day: a steady wind but not too strong. . . .

Here no rain is likely, unless, as so often happens, our most beautiful summer days turn dark and violent in late afternoon, thunderstorms pelting us with rain or hail. I think of a friend who was dying, who had saved up all her laundry for my visit. "I can't trust my husband with it," she whispered conspiratorially. "Men don't understand that clothes must be hung on a line."

She was right. Hanging up wet clothes gives me time alone under the sky to think, to grieve, and gathering the clean clothes in, smelling the sunlight on them, is victory.

KATHLEEN NORRIS
Dakota: A Spiritual Geography

Edith Vonnegut, *Hanging the Laundry,* 1992

Samantabhadra is the shining practice Bodhisattva. She turns meditation into action and dream into reality. We tend to think there is someone out there to help us do this, but unfolding the path completely depends on ourselves. When we become Samantabhadra herself we can freely ride this wheel of dharma and receive wonderful support from people, friends, and teachers.

MAYUMI ODA
Goddesses

When we remember the Goddess and the old earth-based religion, we come back into contact with cycles and the eternal return that lets us face death without fear. It wasn't until 400 CE that the Christian church declared that there were no cycles, no reincarnation. Until that time, everyone knew the obvious, that there certainly is life after death, and it is not only in the eternal realm. One of the joyous reclaimings that accompanies our re-membering is that we get over the insidious fear of the Death Goddess and realize she is only the other face of the Mother. In surrender to her, we leave the problem in her hands; in allowing ourselves to be used in the healing of the planet, we become part of her solution.

VICKI NOBLE
Shakti Woman

Jane Lund, *Self-Portrait with Skull,* 1977

I am the poet of the woman the same as the man,
And I say it is as great to be a woman as to be a man,
And I say there is nothing greater than the mother of men.

WALT WHITMAN
from *Song of Myself*

Christopher Gowell, *Barefoot, Pregnant and on a Pedestal,* 1991

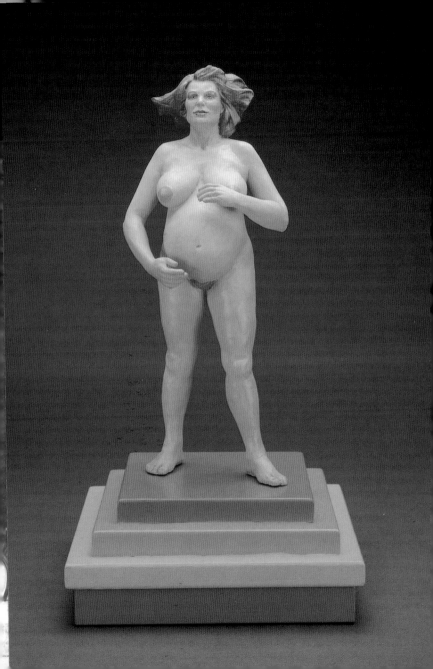

Watching the moon
at dawn,
solitary, mid-sky,
I knew myself completely,
no part left out.

IZUMI SHIKIBU
The Ink Dark Moon
translated by Jane Hirshfield
and Mariko Aratami

Imogen Cunningham, *Shen Yao, Professor of Linguistics
at the University of Hawaii, 1938*

Mother consciousness makes women aware that their bodies and lives are the thread and web that connects all of humanity. And that web is boundless. Because she is in the image of the Cosmic Mother Goddess, a woman's sexuality and creative powers also reflect the divine life-giving, nourishing energies and powers of the universe.

DONNA WILSHIRE
VIRGINMotherCRONE

We call our forebearers ancestors; but in a sense our child-
hood being is our nearest ancestor. A few years ago at a
women's festival, I watched a poignant dance called "A Woman
Giving Birth to Herself." For the dance, one moment of emergence and new awareness had been chosen, but the dancer and
all of us knew that the dance is going on all the time. If we are
alive and growing, we are continuously giving birth to ourselves.

ELSA GIDLOW
ELSA: I Come With My Songs

Judy Dater, *Child / Woman,* 1991

Since a woman's body, which is so like the earth, makes enough food for her offspring, our early ancestors learned to trust the Mother, fashioning images of this Great Mother with large, abundant breasts and a full, pregnant belly. For millennia—maybe since the beginning of consciousness—the community of these women and their male and female offspring loved, thanked, and sang praises to this earth. Most modern archaeology dates the Venus figurines to around 25,000 BCE, but recent British research points to a date for the earliest Great Goddess figures of up to three million years ago—the very dawn of human evolution. The earliest humans created images of the divine woman from stone, the forms of which still, amazingly, survive.

VICKI NOBLE
Shakti Woman

Cheri Gaulke, video production still from *Revelations of the Flesh,* 1985

Most ancient symbol systems recognized the triangle as a sign of the Goddess's Virgin-Mother-Crone trinity and at the same time as her genital "holy place," source of all life. The triangle represented the Virgin Moon Goddess called Men-Nefer, archaic deity of the first Mother-city of Memphis. The triangle itself was worshipped in much the same way that modern Christians worship the cross.

BARBARA WALKER
The Woman's Encyclopedia of Myths and Secrets

Pre-Raphaelite nude study, circa 1920

The dog as the keeper of Mother's gate was known everywhere in antiquity, probably because wild dogs were first domesticated as guardians of the home threshold, doorways being generally sacred to women who owned the houses.

BARBARA WALKER
The Woman's Encyclopedia of Myths and Secrets

Edwin McCarton, *Diana and Hound, circa 1925*

Hera seems to have been one of the Ten Thousand Names of the Great Mother Goddess, the Creatrix, who was revered over vast areas in pre-history. It is likely that originally *Hera* translated as "air" and "sky," indicating essential life-giving, overarching Presence much like Mother Nut in Egypt. . . . Eventually *Hera* was used as a title for the Goddess, meaning something like Great Lady, Protectress, Esteemed Beloved One. In matristic times Her name, like the Sumerian Goddess Inanna's, was incorporated into Her peoples' lives and Selves and was used as if it were synonymous with the words "womb," "woman," "temple," "house," "vessel."

DONNA WILSHIRE
Virgin Mother Crone

Janet McKenzie, *Mother Bird,* 1992

HOUSING SHORTAGE

I tried to live small.
I took a narrow bed.
I held my elbows to my sides.
I tried to step carefully
And to think softly
And to breathe shallowly
In my portion of air
And to disturb no one.

Yet see how I spread out and
        I cannot help it.
I take to myself more and more,
        and I take nothing
That I do not need, but
        my needs grow like weeds.
All over and invading,
        I clutter this place
With all the apparatus
        of living.
You stumble over it daily.

And then my lungs
        take their fill.
And then you gasp for air.
Excuse me for living.
But, since I am living,
Given inches, I take yards,
Taking yards, dream of miles,
And a landscape, unbounded
And vast in abandon.

And, you dreaming the same.

NAOMI REPLANSKY

Sigmund Abeles, *My Love Asleep,* 1989

Settle for
Settle for nothing
Settle for nothing less
Settle for nothing less than

Settle for nothing
less than the
object of your
desire.

Desire. The weight of. The weight of our
desire. Then laugh, cry, but laugh
more than you cry, and when you hold
the world in your hands, love Her.

ALMA LUZ VILLANUEVA
from "The Object"

William Holman Hunt, *The Lady of Shalott,* ca. 1886–1905

For many women, one of the signs of the emergence of goddess energy is strange dreams in which an animal or animals play an important role. In the ancient shamanic traditions, animals came in dreams as powerful allies. For us in the modern world, these animal helpers have lain dormant for many centuries. But they are returning and bringing with them powerful assistance if we pay attention to our dream life. One such animal helper is the snake. The ancient companion of the Great Mother, the snake carries messages about the subtle energies of the earth. Turtles, bears, horses, and raccoons are all common animal helpers that bring subtle assistance through our dreams.

JENNIFER BARKER WOOLGER and ROGER J. WOOLGER
The Goddess Within

The matriarchal deity is not the Great Mother in heaven or any-where else. Rather, she is always concrete and present, visible and touchable. For she *is* the earth humankind is living on, and she *is* the cosmos we can see shining above us in the sky. This goddess is never alien or elevated or superior, because she also *is* the network of spiritual, intellectual, psychic and physical powers within us.

HEIDE GÖTTNER-ABENDROTH
from "Thou Gaia Art I"

Edward Burne-Jones, *The Mirror of Venus*

I want to take life by the horns as if it were a young bull, but I won't stab it in the flank nor pass a sword through its throat nor thrust myself over the horns, not that, but I will dance with it, dance with the awkward bull. Dance.

DEENA METZGER
from *Tree & The Woman Who Slept with Men*
to Take the War Out of Them

Nancy Fried, *The Flirt,* 1987

The magical rebirth of the Goddess today can only mean that the Mother is ready to be healed by our acts of love and caring, by our songs of praise, by our celebration of Her fertility, by our recognition of Her power, and by the energy we invest in re-membering Her beauty, Her strength, Her wisdom, Her life force, and Her bounty. The flourishing of a feminist matristic vision today is a sign that it may not be too late to save our Mother's life.

GLORIA FEMAN ORENSTEIN
The Reflowering of the Goddess

The Old Woman is our beginnings and our endings, and our beginnings again. Enriched by the experiences of living, she is the missing link in the sacred circle.

JEANNE BROOKS CARRITT
"Our Bodies Are Still Sacred as We Age"

Jane Bregoli, *The Goat Lady Series, #2*, 1990

It was nearly seven thousand
    years ago
in Central Bulgaria
that an artist
took the earthy clay
    into her hands
and sculpted a pregnant goddess,
then placed her in
    the temple oven,
perhaps with a prayer
for the endless fields,
fertile and moist.

Now you are enthroned
    on my desk,
face tilted up,
hands resting on
    the divine belly.
As I sit before you,
    I am nauseated,
a waste dump site like
    so much of the earth now.
I do not trust anything.
Still, the moon began again
    last night.

If I pulled down the copper
    blinds and rested in the
    dark,
if I placed you upon
    my patch of dark hair,
would you love me always
    as only a spirit could do?
Would I feel a pulse rise
    from a coiled damp place?
Lady of Pazardzik,
what is behind those
    thumbprint eyes?
I touch you as if
    I were blind.
My late start makes
    the day fall down
      all around me.
Will you carry me over
    the sacred sown fields,
wet fields of imagination?
Sprout me, grow me, let me
    ripen,
but most of all, use me
    for something!
    Use me

STARR GOODE
from "Lady of Pazardzik"

Nancy Blair, Star River Productions, *The Enthroned Goddess,* 1988,
Reproduction of the Bulgarian original (ca. 550 BCE)

When I dance, the sun sails safely through the night.
When I dance, the future is formed by my feet.
When I dance, the stars move through the heavens . . .
When I dance, Venus shimmers the desert,
When I dance, dust becomes silver, stones are made of gold.

COSI FABIAN
from "Hierodule"

Don Manza, *Frances Alenikoff, Trine*

CHOICE

INANNA AND THE GALLA

Helpless on a meathook
she hangs naked:

the circle of her belly reflects the Sun Above;
her necklace droops below her belly button;

down-drawing
elongates her fingers
melts her feet into the pit;

the galla gloat and drool into the Great Below:

her eyes open.

PEM KREMER

Gregory Gillespie, *White Goddess*, 1990

VI. MYTH OF RETURN

White Lady of death,
lover carved of bone,
take me inside your stiff embrace.
Or will you appear as a bird or a snake,
perhaps a beautiful woman.

Lady with no eyes,
take this death
into your chrysalis belly.
The magic womb makes life
come again, in the rising
spring morning.

STARR GOODE
from "Water Movements"

Janet McKenzie, *The Realization of Exile,* 1990

It is the Great Goddess that initiates us into the profound mysteries of creation. Each time we enter into a creative act we open ourselves again to her rhythms, and to the great cycle of fragmentation, death and burial, self-seeding, and regeneration.

PATRICIA REIS
Through the Goddess: A Woman's Way of Healing

Judy Dater, *Imogen and Twinka,* 1974

WORD MAGIC

hag (hag) n. 1. an ugly old woman, esp. a vicious or malicious one.
2. a witch

hagio-, a learned borrowing from Greek meaning "saint," "holy,"
"sacred," used in the formation of compound words:
hagiology, hagiocracy

hagiocracy (hag′ e ok′ r se) n. 1. government by a body of persons
esteemed as holy

BURLEIGH MUTÉN

Deidre Scherer, *Saint,* 1992

She is the rescuer from every danger and peril, the advisor for every tight spot, and the highest wisdom. The people's chiefs and leaders, as well as the whole people itself, are advised by her; she presides over all local, tribal, and national gatherings. She maintains life and health. She is the gracious, gentle nurse who takes the children of mankind to herself, who makes mothers fertile and children grow and develop, who increases the stock of the people through a strong younger generation. She preserves the divine order in nature, protects the seedlings and fruits from damage, sows and tends the noble and nourishing olive trees. She teaches men how to manufacture and plow, how to yoke oxen, and how to loosen up the hard ground with a rake. From her mankind receives the materials for all the arts that beautify life, and from her their skillfulness.

KARL KERÉNYI
Athene: Virgin and Mother in Greek Religion

Irene Young, *Athena*, 1990

In the young spring evening
The moon is shining full
Girls form a circle
As though round an altar

And their feet perform
Rhythmical steps
Like the soft feet of
     Cretan girls
Must once have danced

Round and round
     an altar of love
Designing a circle
In the delicate flowering grass

The stars that are shining
Around the beautiful moon
Hide their own bright faces

When She, at Her fullest
Paints the earth with Her
Silvery light

Now, while we are dancing
Come! Join us!
Sweet joy, revelry,
Bright light!

Inspire us, muses
Oh, you with the beautiful hair.

SAPPHO
verses 22–25
translated by Charoula

Jim Schlessinger, *Lillian, 1992*

BURIALS

What if, a millennium from
    now, you
are exhumed dressed
    completely in gold,
every limb, every finger
    encircled with sun
metal twisted into snakes
    and flowers?

What if they find you wrapped
    in a shroud
of silver meshed like spider
    webs? Or covered
with a boulder big as yourself?
    Or beheaded,
your skull set in a niche
    to hold candles,
a sconce behind you like a halo?

What if they find that you
    were burned, and
traces of the ceremony show
    it was at dusk,
and that you rode a chariot
    or a boat
into the afterlife? Or if
    they find threads
of a cocoon that held you,
    the only thing except
your bones to survive so long?
    If so, what
would they say? This is
    the body of a woman
hale but bent with age,
    this is the body
of a woman who bore
    many children,

this is the body of a woman
    who lost
several teeth, this is
    the body of a woman
who lived on chestnuts and
    occasional lambs' meat?

This is the body of a woman,
they would say, and
from a millennium of death
how could you say back:

Not just a young girl dead
    in childbirth but
a woman blasted from
    the impact of creation,
not just a woman
    in her prime but
a mother of the tribe, not just

an old woman but
    a hallowed elder,
not a woman but a priest,
not a woman but a queen,
not a woman but a vessel for
the energy of Goddess?

This is what they hide from us:
forty thousand years ago
    a crone was buried
nested in the arms of
    her young lover
who killed himself upon
    her death.

Behold, behold.

PATRICIA MONAGHAN

The Goddess in all her manifestations was a symbol of the unity of all life in Nature. Her power was in water and stone, in tomb and cave, in animals and birds, snakes and fish, hills, trees, and flowers. Hence the holistic and mythopoeic perception of the sacredness and mystery of all there is on Earth.

. . . The Goddess gradually retreated into the depths of forests or onto mountaintops, where she remains to this day in beliefs and fairy stories. Human alienation from the vital roots of earthly life ensued, the results of which are clear in our contemporary society. But the cycles never stop turning, and now we find the Goddess reemerging from the forests and mountains, bringing us hope for the future, returning us to our most ancient human roots.

MARIJA GIMBUTAS
The Language of the Goddess

Bodhisattva Kuan-yin, China, 11th to early 12th century

As a woman, I have no country.
As a woman, I want no country.
As a woman, the whole world is my country.

VIRGINIA WOOLF
Three Guineas

Earth as Seen from 23,000 Miles Away, 1972, NASA/World Perspectives

EPILOGUE

I was raking a path through the woods when the idea of an engagement calendar with images and words about the Goddess occurred to me. I was a full-time mother and housewife at the time, with a battery-run intercom receiver tucked in my pocket so that I could hear my young son awaken from his nap as I raked. I'd never liked raking leaves, but I remember how much pleasure I felt that day uncovering roots that had curled themselves tightly around the mossy granite that anchored them. I liked the symbolism of creating a path. As I pulled my metal rake over thousands of oak leaves, I trusted the symbolic gesture of raking a path, and I believed that somehow that action on the hillside in my backyard would become a metaphor for finding my way in life.

After thirteen years of touting the integrity of mothering as meaningful work in the midst of a feminist era, I'd recently begun to feel the lonely but comfortable weight of invisibility. There was no doubt that I'd grown into my power by giving birth to a daughter and a son, nurturing and protecting their talents and preparing them to live effectively out in the world.

But before I was a mother, when I was still a girl in high school, I'd discovered my own strong voice as a writer, but I still hadn't taken her out into the world. I was in my early forties, and I'd worked as a teacher and a technical editor, and I'd helped start two schools and one magazine, but deep inside I knew there was something more for me, something I was still afraid to claim. I held a ferocious belief in motherhood, but for the first time in my life I began to see my parenting as energy ultimately spent in behalf of someone else. I still needed to mother myself.

I knew that day as I raked, smiling at the beauty of the strong roots that moments before had been covered by seasons of change, that I knew how to take an idea and make it into a book, and deep down, I knew it was a good idea. If I didn't do it, someone else would.

The week before, as I read *The Goddess Within* (by Jennifer B. and Roger Woolger) during naptime, I was full of pride when I discovered that motherhood was once considered sacred. Right here on earth, several thousands of years ago, a pregnant woman was sacred, a mother divine!

And when I read that the ancient goddesses were thought of as agents of transformation, I realized how much I ached for transformation. The truth was that mothering had offered me a grand vehicle for growth, but it wasn't the full expression of my creativity. I needed to use my own voice out in the world. I was tired of being invisible, but I didn't know how to be visible, and what's more, I was terrified of what that might mean for me.

The more I read about ancient matristic cultures, the more excited I became. Just knowing that the priestesses of Delphi had guided the politics of their times stirred something inside me. And discovering that the sexual priestesses in Sumeria and Egypt were the initiators of young men prior to marriage as well as agents for healing was an affirmation of the goodness of my body that I'd never felt before.

I took the goddess quiz in the Woolgers' book, and predictably, Demeter, the mother in my personality, scored off the chart while the leader of women, Hera the Queen, barely registered any score, so undeveloped was she within me. But I could invoke her, I could ask for her help just as women did during the days when every household had altars to women.

So when I was vacuuming one day and the words "Long ago before the wars, Hera was our mother" surfaced in my mind, I held on to them. For weeks after that, I recited that line, trying out the rhythm and words that might follow, crafting a lyric poem, longer and unlike anything I'd ever written. I read everything I could get my hands on to find out who Hera was before she was shaped into a secondary figure in Zeus's pantheon. I felt so strong writing that poem, I wanted all women to know what I was finding out about.

I phoned an old editing colleague, Peggy Ann White, a visual artist in her late thirties who also yearned to manifest her creative voice. She agreed that an engagement calendar would reach a lot of women. I told her what I knew about the market for it—there was nothing like it out there. "But I couldn't do it alone, Peg. Will you do it with me?"

I didn't know it then, but what I was asking for was belief in my idea and a hand to hold as I leaped off the cliff into the abyss. I had a sense that it was time for this information to become more widely known, and I trusted that the Goddess would help me. I was simply terrified of starting a business and of owning my power out in the world without a constant ally.

Whenever I got scared, I calmed my fear by reading goddess books, researching for the calendar. Everything I read felt like Old Truth as familiar and profound as my newborns had felt the first time I held them in my arms. I began to light up with hope as I realized what the return of this knowledge about women could mean for the planet. This could be it. This could be my contribution.

For the next six months I drove to Peggy's cottage in Connecticut once a month to work on the calendar. We had read about women's rituals, but since neither of us had ever been to one, we improvised. With *The Spiral Dance* (by Starhawk) sitting in one of our laps for quick reference, we lit a candle in the middle of Peggy's kitchen table and called to the four directions, and the nine muses who govern the arts, and all the goddesses we knew of at that time. Around the candle we placed photos of our grandmothers and postcards and Xeroxes of images we hoped to include in the calendar. I read my Queen Hera poem, and then we talked about how we'd format the calendar, what size it should be, what goddesses would be included, what holidays and astrology should be included, its title, what quotes and which artists might be right for it.

I had pasted an image of Gaia holding two nursing children in her arms on the cover of a blank book in which I took notes. Before we'd close our sacred space, I'd place the book on the altar next to my fountain pen and Peggy's best sable brush. And we'd sing, "In the stillness of the night, we are making our dreams come true," a song I'd learned from my daughter, who had learned it at camp that summer.

I began calling national book distributors who handle the majority of calendar sales throughout the country, to try out the idea on them. "Date book on the Goddess? Color reproductions? Fine art? Sounds great. Send sample pages as soon as you have them," they all said.

It was February 1991—too late for the 1992 calendar season. We were amazed, and we were relieved. We laughed at ourselves.

We knew we had a lot to find out. We needed a year to find our way.

I started telling my friends about the calendar. They were excited for me. "Here's the name of an excellent graphic designer," Barbara said as she handed me a business card. I'd never heard of graphic design, I had no idea what a graphic designer did, but I thanked her and placed it on the shelf next to my desk.

Two weeks later, Glenn Ruga, the excellent graphic designer, happened to be standing next to me in the coffee line at the deli. After a few moments of conversation, I realized the synchronicity of this friendly young man appearing at my side and, bolstered by the apparent coincidence (was it a gift from the Goddess?), introduced myself.

"I've heard of you," I said, and explained the reference made by our mutual friend. "I'm designing and hoping to produce an engagement calendar with the theme of women's spirituality, with quotes and fine art reproductions," I told him. Still figuring I could handle the design myself, I asked him about printers. He mentioned a few, handed me another one of his cards, and I promised to phone for an appointment in a few weeks when he would return from Europe. I figured that any professional who knew how to put this puzzle together would be my teacher. And there was something genuine in his smile when I mentioned women's spirituality.

Before Glenn returned from his trip, I'd met with three printers. The first could hardly take me seriously—I knew so little about the specifications of the book and nothing about the printing process. The second and third printers were more direct; both recommended graphic design, and they both recommended Glenn.

But how could I evaluate a graphic designer? I knew how to interview teachers and babysitters, but I barely knew the steps involved in designing and printing a book. It had been years since I'd edited professionally. I interviewed three designers, explained what I wanted the calendar to be, looked at their portfolios, asked hundreds of questions, and requested an estimate. All three were obviously talented and competent.

The only real tool I had with which to choose was the feeling in my gut: my intuition. For the first time in my life, I was aware of a visceral sensation in the center of my body as a *reliable* means of knowing what choice to make. I'd certainly been reading a lot about women's wisdom, women's ways of knowing, and the importance of trusting what our own bodies tell us. I was proud to make an important business decision from a message from within my own body. I chose Glenn Ruga, the excellent graphic designer my friend had recommended.

It felt good to have a man involved on the project. As the mother of a son and a daughter, I can't help wanting this healing symbol of the goddess to influence both genders. We all live on Earth. Women, men, and Gaia need this resource of the ancient Feminine.

Peggy and I had decided on a name for the calendar, *Return of the Goddess;* a name for the business, Hands of the Goddess Press; and a graphic designer. The time had come when we needed financial backing. We each put a fifty-dollar bill on the altar that month, and I read the business plan I'd written. We called on Hecate, the Greek goddess of the crossroads, to guide us that night because we knew we were about to enter the place of no turning back.

That week I phoned my mother-in-law, Jet Mutén, who had introduced me to the Great Goddess several years before, and who had once owned a business, to invite her to be our silent partner. We'd decided to fund-raise for a year if she didn't want to get involved. We might have to wait another year for publication, but maybe we wouldn't mind that either.

"No, I don't want to own a business right now," Jet replied. "But I'd be glad to loan you the money. How much do you need, dear?"

It was that easy, one phone call! I hung up, stunned, and called Peggy. We screamed with excitement and terror. We were in the air now, right over the abyss.

That night I dreamed about Rich Michelson, who owns the art gallery in town. I was telling Rich about the calendar when John and Yoko walked up to us. "Tell John about the calendar," Rich said to me.

Sure, John Lennon would have been part of the goddess movement, I thought to myself. Yoko and John's peace campaigns and many of his last songs spoke of the ethics of women's spirituality. I'd always loved their work. So I wrote her a letter describing the calendar and invited her to submit her work. There was nothing to lose in asking.

A few weeks later I stopped in at the R. Michelson Gallery to inquire about how I might contact Carol Grigg, whose watercolors of Native American women would be perfect for the calendar. I'd always felt shy around Rich, whom I'd known until then as a fellow parent. He's tall and thin and often quiet, like me, so we'd rarely spoken. When I told him about the calendar, his smile broadened. He had a lot to say. "Have you seen Leonard Baskin's Sybil series?" and "Do you know Mark Weiss's work?" and "Yes, I sure do know of a painting of the Statue of Liberty."

I left the gallery with five artists added to the roster and an ally. Smiles, smiles all around. It was Friday the thirteenth. "In the darkness of the night, in the darkness of the moon, I am making my dreams come true," I sang all the way to my son's preschool and all the way home.

I was at the sink snapping peas one afternoon, my son watching "Sesame Street" in the next room, when the phone rang. It was Carol Grigg! "I got your letter last week, and I just wanted to call to thank you for doing this work for all of us." She was so friendly that I decided to be candid, and I told her that I'd never done anything like this before, that this project was the metaphor for my own transformation as a woman. "You have plenty of time, plenty of time. Look at me, I started painting ten years ago when I was forty, and I am surrounded by so much abundance now. When you come from your heart, you can't lose. This is a brilliant idea."

I was high for a week, being encouraged like that by a successful woman artist. Then Judy Chicago replied yes. And Judy Dater and Gregory Gillespie and Jane Lund. And Yoko! From listening to my own dream, I could include the work of one of my heroines in this work of mine. From remembering and listening to a dream . . . from honoring my own inner wisdom!

Spec sheets of the calendar were sent out to printers for bids. And again, I had to let my body guide me. Glenn provided the expert advice I needed, but the decision was, after all, mine. My intuition was the best resource I had; I trusted it. I chose a local printer with a fine reputation, which meant I could witness the process and begin to learn about this vast dimension of a publisher's responsibilities.

The calendar began to feel like a blessed and destined project. I was just the lucky woman making the arrangements for it. Not to say that I wasn't doing an enormous amount of personal homework. In between the vibrant validations, I plummeted into screeching self-doubt and fear. Nothing in my life had ever brought such regular, consistent affirmation. And nothing had ever brought such regular, consistent anxiety.

What was I terrified of? It was hard to articulate the forces behind the feelings that jolted me awake night after night. I'd been shy all my life. But I never realized until I chose this work that behind the shyness stood fear of rejection, exclusion, criticism, anger, even physical harm.

I never knew until I put myself in the hands of the Goddess that I'd been afraid all these years. I'd been playing it safe as an innovative parent and teacher, funneling my creativity and risk-taking spirit into the future through other human beings. I'd always advocated for the self-esteem and creative expression of children. My own self-esteem was so wounded, I didn't even know how frightened I was.

I silenced my fear by going to work. There was always something to do, something new to find out about. So when my belly started churning, I phoned up the copyright office to find out about that procedure or contacted an attorney to draw up a contract to use with the artists or went to the library to research an image.

One night, my eyes sprung open. I didn't even remember the dream I'd had. I turned on the light, opened my journal, and wrote down a list of affirmations, starting with the one my yoga teacher always uses to begin the guided relaxation. "I am a woman, a human being of extraordinary strength, wisdom, and grace." And I went on: "I am a publisher, the hands of the goddess are my hands, I am a mother, a writer, a teacher, I am an entrepreneur, I am a strong warrior, I am a risk-taker, I am a leader, a woman with ideas that are welcome in these times on this planet."

I said this prayer every night before I went to sleep, and I said it whenever I woke startled and afraid. It became the voice of the motherBurl, reminding the timid littlegirlBurl who'd forgotten herself. I'd say it until I fell asleep like a lullaby.

In one dream, a Neolithic goddess figure sits before me. She has no eyes, a bird nose, chevrons creased into her chest and on her skirt, her hands resting on her belly. As I look at her, I become her. Sensing my body as one does when one's eyes are closed, I can hear but I cannot see. As I sit in blind stillness, I am comfortable within the limits of my shape.

"That's a first! Dreaming in Neolithic!" I thought to myself, startled awake one more time. "I wonder who that goddess is. I know I've seen her in one of my books. I'll look her up tomorrow." As I contemplated being a goddess without eyes, I wondered what I didn't want to see. And then the rest of the dream flooded in.

It's wartime in an elegant European city. I'm walking through a long, narrow cobblestone corridor, flanked by attached buildings, that leads into the center of the city where the Queen lives. The streets are crammed with terrified people hurrying toward the Imperial Palace plaza, where thousands of people have always gathered for state occasions. Today they move with speed and urgency amid the military on horseback.

Word spreads through the crowd that enemy tanks are journeying through the labyrinth of the palace corridor, and the tide turns. Everyone begins to flee the city, and I follow the flow away from the Queen's palace. Huge, indifferent tanks push the crowd aside.

I am four or five, lost and scared and curious and excited. This is the first time I've ever been alone out in the world. The fear in the crowd and the tanks roaring so close scare me. I begin to follow an old woman whose skin is like mine, deep, glowing brown. I follow at a distance, then closer. She gets on a train, packed with the lucky, horrified ones who are on their way away from danger, and I follow her onto the train. I never take my eyes from her. She is my promise of safety.

She rises to get off the train. I'm right behind her. Turning, she looks down at me, and I'm afraid she will leave me. "Take me, take me with you," I plead. "Don't leave me." She opens her arms, picks me up, and carries me off the train. I am big for her to carry, but we grip each other. Her arms are strong and her body is soft. She lumbers down the steps of the train out into the daylight and carries me home.

This was no ordinary dream. The smell of that woman's big, soft body pressed against mine was as real as the bed I lay in. Staring at the stars overhead, I replayed the dream in my mind. As I saw her hands reaching for my small torso, I began to cry. Tears flooded my cheeks so fast that I shook with sorrow, bursting into sobs that woke my husband.

"What's the matter?" Erik asked, opening his arms to me.

I cried for a long time before I could tell him. It was a deep, grieving sort of cry, my whole body shaking.

"You're such a smart woman," he whispered into my hair again and again. "So smart and brave. You've found a way to say what you see, and you're giving it to thousands of women. Of course the Goddess didn't leave you behind."

In a comparative literature class at the local university, I read about Inanna, the Sumerian goddess whose sister, the Queen of the Dead, stripped her naked of all jeweled adornment and hung her corpse on a meat hook on the wall. I could identify with this story. I had willingly journeyed down into the dark where my fear waited to impale me.

Day after day I walked through one door after another into the unknown territory where publishers walk. Night after night the decisions I made by day, navigating my way to self-actualization, were played out like the theater of the ancients. I shaped a little statue of Inanna one afternoon with my son's purple Play-Doh. Inanna returned from the land of the dead. I could make it too.

When Starhawk and Margot Adler led workshops on women's spirituality nearby, I couldn't resist. I had to find out how ritual was done by those who "knew."

Margot asked each of us to introduce ourselves by placing a special object on the star-dotted, deep blue altar cloth that had been spread in the center of the circle. Still timid and scared, I stood slowly and walked to the altar of crystals and flowers and goddess figures and photos, and placed my new business card next to a huge pine cone. I turned to face all these women, the largest group I'd ever addressed, maybe a hundred women. I looked out at their faces, eager to know me, and I was amazed: safety washed over me. I told them about my business, proudly explaining its name, asked for their visualization that it succeed, and admitted that I'd never had a business card before.

I danced with Starhawk and over a hundred other women in a spiral dance, circling and singing and facing these women I'd gotten to know deeply during the two days we spent together. I saw the respect Starhawk held for the wisdom within each of us. I felt a profound sense of freedom to be me. I could move from the deepest energy in my pelvis as I danced. It was easy to feel that we were all part of history, returning for change. In a chorus of one hundred and fifty voices, I sang for peace and safety on Earth.

One night I dreamed I discovered a whole new wing in my own house, a secret wing that the previous owners hadn't told us about. I was delighted looking at the big old rolltop desk in this attic-type space. It was stuffed with papers, among them a photo of an old woman with wild white hair and eyes that made me feel naked.

The next morning I had an appointment with a photographer who was scheduled to shoot my photo for the press. I arrived early, and her young son needed some attention. "Why don't you look through my portfolio," she suggested. "You might find something suitable for your calendar."

"Who *is* this?" I called into the next room. "Who is this old woman?" On the wizened, kind face of a woman well into her eighties, I met the eyes I'd seen in my dream.

"It's Fräulein Himmler, my photography mentor, who only taught women. She died several years ago."

Okay, I said to myself. I'd just finished shipping the '93 calendar to distributors, but I knew instantly I would have to put Fräulein Himmler into the '94 roster of goddesses.

I began to get used to this sort of "finding magic" as I collected images and quotes for the calendar. One artist often led me to another. Sometimes I walked into the library and, more often than not, within minutes I'd find gold. I began to look at my research as a treasure hunt.

A feeling of honor settled into the deep parts of me. To be part of the women's movement, touching thousands of women's lives every day of their year's experience, shocked and soothed the little-girlBurl who'd been hiding her light all these years. Women began to write to me; people in my hometown began to stop me on the street to thank me for my work.

Well into the second calendar's production, I began to struggle with the decision of not publishing a third one. *Return of the Goddess* had, after all, been a child and a mother to me. But I was ready for the next transformation. And when Samuel Bercholz of Shambhala

Publications phoned to confirm his interest in publishing a book version of the two calendars and more, I took it as one of those signs I'd become used to. This was the nod. She'd prepared me, almost tricked me into owning my own power as a thinker and creative woman out in the world for everyone to see.

Five years ago, when a woman asked me, "When did you first hear the voice of the Goddess?" I couldn't answer. Now I know it was the voice in my own head that's always wanted me to express the best of me. It's the voice I first heard in high school that's been urging me to write ever since. It's the voice I grew to dread, I felt so guilty and fearful at its urging.

I remember asking my mentor, my mother-in-law, who'd introduced me to the Great Goddess, the woman who'd believed in me and blessed my path, "Does the fear ever stop? When will I believe in myself enough that I'm not scared all the time?" She smiled, running her long fingers through her soft white hair. "Never, dear, you just recognize it, look it in the eye, and keep on moving. We can't banish the dark, but we can navigate there, can't we?"

CREDITS

Images

• Abeles, Sigmund. *My Love Asleep.* Oil on panel. 14" x 16". 1989. Collection of the artist.

• Anderson, Judith. *Re-member Us.* Etching. Sepia Ink. 18" x 24". Fall Equinox 1990. Courtesy R. Michelson Galleries, Amherst and Northampton, Mass. (413) 586-3964.

• Azara, Nancy. *Witchspell.* Carved and painted wood with goldleaf. 22" x 14". 1989. Collection: Everson Museum, Syracuse, N.Y. Photo: Erik Lansberg.

• Baskin, Leonard. *Ruth and Naomi.* Watercolor and gouache. 22½" x 30". 1991. Courtesy R. Michelson Galleries, Amherst and Northampton, Mass. (413) 586-3964. Photo: Stephen Petegorsky.

• Baskin, Leonard. *Sybil with Crow.* Watercolor on paper. 22½" x 30". 1991. Courtesy R. Michelson Galleries, Amherst and Northampton, Mass. (413) 586-3964. Photo: Stephen Petegorsky.

• Benton, Suzanne. *The Seer.* 1987. Metal ask and ritual sculpture. Steel and bronze brazed. 23½" x 13¼" x 2½". Courtesy of the artist.

• Blair, Nancy. *The Enthroned Goddess.* Bonded stone. 7½"H. 1988. The Great Goddess Collection, Star River Produc-

tions, PO Box 510642, Melbourne Beach, FL 32951.

• *Bodhisattva Kuan-yin.* Polychromed wood. 95" x 65". Chinese, 11th-early 12th century. The Nelson-Atkins Museum of Art, Kansas City, Mo. Purchase: Nelson Trust.

• Bredin-Price, Joan. *Drawing Down the Moon.* Gouache. 1992. Photo: Stephen Petegorsky.

• Bregoli, Jane. *Crepuscule in Black and Brown:Wendy.* Watercolor. © 1993. 41" x 32". Courtesy of the artist.

• Bregoli, Jane. *The Goat Lady Series, #2.* Oil on canvas. 60" x 40". 1990. Courtesy of the artist. Lithographs of this image are available.

• Burne-Jones, Edward. *The Mirror of Venus.* Gulbenkian Museum, Lisbon. Reproduced by permission of Bridgeman/Art Resource, NY.

• Carrey, Bobbi. *Terra Firma, 1974.* © 1995 by Bobbi Carrey. Reproduced by permission of the artist.

• Catlett, Elizabeth. *Three Women of America.* Silkscreen. 34" x 28". 1990. Reproduced by permission of the artist.

• Chicago, Judy. *Sappho* plate from *The Dinner Party*. China—paint on porcelain. 14" diameter. © 1979 by Judy Chicago. Photo © by Donald Woodman.

• Chicago, Judy. *The Crowning* from *The Birth Project*. Needlepoint, 40½" x 61". © 1984 by Judy Chicago. Needlepoint by Frannie Yablonsky. Photo © by Michele Maier.

• Cunningham, Imogen. *Martha Graham 2*, 1931. © 1974, 1994 by The Imogen Cunningham Trust. All rights reserved.

• Cunningham, Imogen. *Shen Yao, Professor of Linguistics at the University of Hawaii 1938*. © 1970, 1994 by The Imogen Cunningham Trust. All rights reserved.

• Dater, Judy. *Imogen and Twinka*. © 1974 by Judy Dater. Reproduced by permission of the artist.

• Dater, Judy. *Child/Woman*. © 1991 by Judy Dater. Reproduced by permission of the artist.

• de Buhr, Evelyn. Left panel from *Bathers Triptych*. 30" x 48". 1990. Courtesy of Evelyn de Buhr, PO Box 158, Hanalei, HI 96714.

• *Earth as Seen from 23,000 Miles Away*, 1972. NASA image courtesy of World Perspectives, San Rafael, Calif.

• Feshbach, Oriole Farb. *Megan Inspired by a Renaissance Portrait*. 1977. 28" x 20". Offset lithograph. By permission of the artist.

• Flack, Audrey. *Colossal Head of Medusa*. Patinated and gilded bronze. 35½" high with base. 1991. Photo courtesy Louis K. Meisel Gallery, N.Y. Photo: Steve Lopez.

• Fried, Nancy. *The Flirt*. Terra cotta. 10¼"

x 13". 1987. Courtesy of the artist.

• Gambaro, Retha. *Daughter of Mother Earth*. Bronze sculpture. 11¾". 1991. Photo: Stephen Gambaro.

• Gaulke, Cheri. Video production still from *Revelations of the Flesh* by Cheri Gaulke. Performer: Sue Maberry. © 1985 by Cheri Gaulke.

• Gillespie, Gregory. White Goddess. Oil, alkyd, pencil on board. 22¾" x 16". 1990. Courtesy of Gregory Gillespie.

• Gimbutas, Marija. Line drawings from *The Language of the Goddess*. Courtesy of Marija Gimbutas.

• Gowell, Christopher. *Barefoot, Pregnant and on a Pedestal*. Polychromed resin. 14" x 6" x 5". © 1991 by Christopher Gowell. Photo: Andrew Edgar. Courtesy R. Michelson Galleries, Amherst and Northampton, Mass. (413) 586-3964.

• Gowell, Christopher. *I'm My Own Guardian Angel*. Terra cotta. 21" x 15" x 18". © 1993 by Christopher Gowell. Photo: Andrew Edgar. Courtesy R. Michelson Galleries, Amherst and Northampton, Mass. (413) 586-3964.

• Grigg, Carol. *Daughters of the Moon*. Courtesy of Carol Grigg.

• Hammid, Hella. *Point of View*. © 1991 by Hella Hammid.

• Hatay, Nona. *Fräulein Berta Himmler*. © 1967. Courtesy of the artist.

• Hill, Elizabeth. *The Source*. Hydrocal and plastic. 22" x 22" x 28". 1991. Courtesy of the artist.

• Hoffman, Martina. *Birthscape II*. Oil on

canvas. 39" x 39". 1988.

• Hunt, William Holman. *The Lady of Sha-lott.* Oil on panel. 44.4 x 34.3 cm. Ca. 1886-1905. Manchester City Art Gallery. Photo courtesy Bridgeman/Art Resource, NY.

• *Isis Suckling Horus.* Egyptian, late period. Louvre, Paris. Foto Marburg/Art Resource, NY.

• Johannsmann, Gabriele. *Sheer Lust.* Carved in steatit after the original paleo-lithic figurine (ca. 20,000 BCE) found in Sir-euil, France. 4" x 1¼". © 1991 by Gabriele Johannsmann. Photo: Jim Schlessinger.

• Johnson, Belle. *Three Women with Long Hair,* ca. 1900. Courtesy of the Massillon Museum of Art, Massillon, Ohio.

• Keiser, Carol. *Virgin de la Salud.* Acrylic on Arches 140 lb. paper. 18" x 24". 1991. Courtesy of the artist.

• Kingston, Rodger. *Cia with Stars, Albuquer-que, NM 1993.* © 1993. Courtesy of the artist.

• Korican, Leah. *Totem.* Oil on canvas. 11" x 14". 1992. Courtesy of the artist.

• Kruger, Deborah. *Namah's Womb.* Artist quilt. 84" x 55". © 1991 by Deborah Kru-ger. Courtesy of the artist. Photo © 1991 by John Polak.

• Kuch, Michael. *The Night Stitcher.* Water-color. 40" x 30". 1991. Courtesy of the R. Michelson Galleries, Amherst and North-ampton, Mass. (413) 586-3964.

• Lachaise, Gaston. *Garden Figure,* ca. 1935. Cast concrete. 79½" x 27½" x 17". Smith College Museum of Art, Northampton,

Mass. Gift of Mrs. Henry T. Curtiss (Mina Kirstein '18), 1982.

• Larsson, Carl. *Model Writing Picture Postals.* 1906. Courtesy of Theilska Galleriet, Stockholm.

• Lund, Jane. *Self-Portrait with Skull.* Pastel. 23" x 32 ¼". 1977. Courtesy of the artist. Photo: Bill Ravanesi.

• Manza, Don. *Frances Alenikoff, Trine.* © 1995 Don Manza. Reprinted by permis-sion of Don Manza and the performer, Frances Alenikoff.

• McCarton, Edwin. *Diana and Hound,* ca. 1925. Photo: Louis Dreyer. Courtesy Rod-ger Kingston Collection, Boston.

• McKenzie, Janet. *Mother Bird.* Oil on can-vas. 40" x 54". Reproduced by permission of the artist. PO Box 681, Colchester, VT 05446.

• McKenzie, Janet. *Purity.* Oil on canvas. 30" x 54". 1992. Reproduced by permis-sion of the artist.

• McKenzie, Janet. *The Realization of Exile.* Oil on canvas. 54" x 54". Reproduced by permission of the artist.

• McKusick, Sarah Chester. *Unfolding Earth.* © 1995 Sarah C. McKusick. By permission of the artist.

• Meunier, Mark. *Statue of Liberty.* Egg tem-pera on board. 22" x 28". 1986. Courtesy R. Michelson Galleries, Amherst and Northampton, Mass. (413) 586-3964.

• Mookerjee, Sudha. *Goddess Kali.* Water-color tempera, 1954. Photo: Priya Mookerjee, N.Y.

• *Nutrix Eius Terra Est / The Earth Is the Nur-*

turer of Us All. Attributed to Theodor deBry, German, 17th century. From Michael Maier, *Atlanta Fugiens, Hoc Est Emblemata Nova de Secretis Naturae Chymica,* Oppenheim Hieronymi Galleri, 1618, p. 17.

• Oda, Mayumi. *Goddess Hears People's Needs and Comes,* from *Goddesses* (Volcano Press). Silkscreen. 24" x 33". 1976. Courtesy of the artist.

• Oda, Mayumi. *Samantabhadra,* from *Goddesses* (Volcano Press). Silkscreen. 29" x 40". 1980. Courtesy of the artist.

• Post, Linda. *Air,* from *The Elements.* Pastel. 50" x 42". 1988. Posters of this image are available from R. Michelson Galleries, Amherst and Northampton, Mass. (413) 586-3964.

• Pre-Raphaelite Nude Study, circa 1920. Photographer unidentified. Courtesy Rodney Kingston Collection, Boston, Mass.

• Ralph, Yohah. *Prostitute, Therapist, and Emerging Woman.* Oil on paper. 42" x 29". © 1991 by Yohah Ralph. Courtesy of the artist. Photo: Stephen Petegosky.

• Ruga, Glenn. From *El Proyecto Holyoke / The Holyoke Project.* Reproduced by permission of the artist.

• Scherer, Deidre. *After Light.* Fabric and thread. 7" x 6½". April 1990. © 1994 by Deidre Scherer. Courtesy of the artist. PO Box 156, Williamsville, VT 05362.

• Scherer, Deidre. *Saint.* Fabric and thread. 7" x 6". July 1992. © 1994. by Deidre Scherer. Courtesy of the artist. Photo: Jeff Baird.

• Schlessinger, Jim. *Lillian, 1992.* Courtesy of the artist.

• Schlessinger, Jim. *Burd and Abby, 1983.* Courtesy of the artist.

• Segal, George. *The Dancers.* Plaster. 56" H. 1971. © 1997 by George Segal / Licensed by VAGA, NY.

• Sevick, *Carol. She Speaks for Peace.* Porcelain. 11" x 7" x 2". January 10, 1991. Courtesy of the artist.

• Shefrin, Roberta Baskin. *The Stranger.* Bronze. 30" H. 1991. Courtesy of the artist.

• Shefrin, Roberta Baskin. *Woman.* Bronze bas relief. 19" x ¾" x 15". 1985. Courtesy of the artist.

• Vonnegut, Edith. *Hanging the Laundry.* Oil on linen. 26" x 22". 1922. Photo: Stephen Petegorsky. Courtesy of the artist.

• Ward, Frank. *Carmen Santiago.* 1990. Courtesy of the artist.

• Weiss, Mark. *Mother Earth.* Acrylic on canvas. 64" x 54". 1990. Courtesy R. Michelson Galleries, Amherst and Northampton, Mass. (413) 586-3964. Posters of this image are available.

• *White Tara.* 17th-century Tibet. 6¾" H. Silver with gold and inlays of copper and semiprecious stones. The Asia Society, N.Y. Mr. and Mrs. John D. Rockefeller 3rd Collection.

• Wronski, Kendrick Anne. *Planting the Seeds.* Acrylic. 48" x 60". 1992. Courtesy of the artist.

• Yarde, Richard. *Josephine Baker Baffle,* center panel of triptych. Watercolor on paper. 41" x 29½". 1992–1993. Photo: Stephen Petegorsky. Courtesy R. Michelson Galleries, Amherst and Northampton, Mass.

(413) 586-3964.

•*Yosemite*, ca. 1900. Photographer unidentified. Courtesy Rodger Kingston Collection, Boston.

•Young, Irene. *Athena.* From the original 24" x 30" photographic creation by Irene Young. © 1990. Courtesy of the artist.

•Young, Irene. *Shakti Woman.* From the original 33" x 28": photographic creation by Irene Young. © 1989. Courtesy of the artist.

•Young, Irene. *Snake Goddess at Knossos.* From the original 30" x 40" photographic creation by Irene Young. ©1989. Courtesy of the artist.

Quotations

•Adler, Margot. From *Drawing Down the Moon* by Margot Adler. Copyright © 1979 by Margot Adler. Used by permission of Viking Penguin, a division of Penguin Books USA, Inc.

•Allen, Paula Gunn. Excerpt from "He Na Tye Woman," in *Shadow Country.* © Regents, University of California, American Indian Research Center, UCLA.

•Allione, Tsultrim. Excerpts from "Sky Dancer," in *woman of power,* no. 15 (1990). Reprinted by permission of the author.

•Anderson, Judith. *Re-member Us.* © 1990. By permission of the author.

•Ardinger, Barbara. *Goddess Meditations.* © 1997 Barbara Ardinger, Ph.D. By permission of the author.

•Austen, Hallie Iglehart. Excerpt from *The Heart of the Goddess: Art, Myth, and Meditations of the World's Sacred Feminine.* © 1990 by Hallie Iglehart Austen, Wingbow Press, Oakland, Calif. Reprinted by permission of the author.

• Barnard, Mary. *Sappho: A New Translation,* verse 46. Copyright © 1958 by The Regents of the University of California. Renewed 1984 by Mary Barnard. Reprinted by permission of the University of California Press.

• Basto, Ronald, trans. Ovid, *Metamorphoses,* and Homer, "Hymn to Selene." © 1994 by Ronald Basto. Reprinted by permission of the translator.

• Benton, Suzanne. "The Second Coming," 1979, to commemorate her NYC Mask and Ritual Procession: Celebrating the Second Coming of the Great Goddess. Suzanne Benton. Reprinted by permission of the author.

• Boer, Charles. "The Hymn to the Earth," in *The Homeric Hymns,* 2nd. rev. ed., trans. Charles Boer (Dallas: Spring Publications, 1979). © 1970 by Charles Bowe. Reprinted by permission of the publisher and author.

• Brindel, June Rachuy. Excerpt from *Ariadne* (New York: St. Martin's Press, 1980). Reprinted by permission of the author.

• Carritt, Jeanne Brooks. Excerpt from "Our Bodies Are Still Sacred as We Age," in *Sacred Dimensions of Women's Experience.* Wellesley, Mass.: Roundtable Press, 1988. Reprinted by permission of the publisher.

• Charoula, trans. Sappho verses 22–25. © 1994 by Charoula. Reprinted by permission of the translator.

• Chicago, Judy. Excerpts from *The Dinner Party.* © 1979 by Judy Chicago.

• Clifton, Lucille. "poem in praise of menstruation" and "to my last period." © 1991 by Lucille Clifton. Reprinted from *Quilting: Poems 1987-1990,* by Lucille Clifton, with the permission of BOA Editions, Ltd, 92 Park Avenue, Brockport, NY 14420.

• Dickinson, Emily. "We never know how high we are." Reprinted by permission of the publishers and the Trustees of Amherst College from *The Poems of Emily Dickinson,* ed. Thomas H. Johnson (Cambridge, Mass.: Belknap Press of Harvard University Press), Copyright © 1951, 1955, 1979, 1983 by the President and Fellows of Harvard College.

• Duerk, Judith. Excerpt from Circle of Stones: Woman's Journey to Herself. Copyright © 1989 by LuraMedia. Reprinted by permission of LuraMedia, Inc., San Diego, Calif.

• Eclipse. Excerpt from "Cicada," from *The Moon in Hand.* Copyright © 1991 by Eclipse. Reprinted by permission of Astarte Shell Press, Portland, Me.

• Estés, Clarissa Pinkola. Excerpts from *Women Who Run with the Wolves.* © 1992 by Ballantine Books, N.Y. Reprinted by permission of Random House, Inc.

• Fabian, Cosi. Excerpt from "Hierodule." © 1990 by Cosi Fabian.

• Feng, Gia-Fu, and Jane English. Excerpt from *Tao Te Ching.* © 1972 by Gia-Fu Feng and Jane English. Reprinted by permission of Alfred A. Knopf, Inc., and Gower Publishing Ltd.

• Getty, Adele. Excerpt from *Goddess.* Copyright © 1990 by Thames and Hudson Ltd. Reprinted by permission of the publisher.

• Gidlow, Elsa. Selection from *ELSA: I Come With My Songs.* Permission courtesy Celeste West and Booklegger Publishing, Box 460654, San Francisco, CA 94146.

• Gimbutas, Marija. Selections from page 321 of *The Language of the Goddess,* copyright © 1989. Reprinted by permission of HarperCollins Publishers, Inc.

• Goode, Starr. Excerpt from "Lady of Pazardzik," © 1989. Excerpt from "Water Movements," © 1989. Reprinted by permission of Starr Goode.

• Goodrich, Norma Lorre. *Priestesses.* Copyright © 1989 by Norma Lorre Goodrich. Reprinted by permission of the publisher, Franklin Watts, Inc., the author, and her agents, Harold Schmidt, Literary Agency.

• Göttner-Abendroth, Heide. Excerpts from "Thou Gaia Art I: Matriachal Mythology in Former Times and Today," *Trivia,* no. 7. PO Box 606, North Amherst, MA 01059. Reprinted by permission of the author.

• Hinckley, Priscilla B. "The New Our Father." © 1995 by Priscilla Hinckley. By permission of the author.

• Hirshfield, J., and M. Aratami, trans. Excerpt from *The Ink Dark Moon.* Copyright © 1990 by Jane Hirshfield and Mariko Aratami. Reprinted by permission of Random House, Inc.

• Kerényi, Karl. *Athene: Virgin and Mother in Greek Religion* (Dallas: Spring Publications, 1978). © 1978 by Spring Publications, Inc.

• Korican, Leah. Excerpt from "City Goddess." Copyright © 1992 Leah Korican. Reprinted by permission of the author.

• Kremer, Pem. "Choice," © 1992 by Pem

Kremer, and "Epiphany," © 1991 by Pem Kremer. Reprinted by permission of the author.

• Kruger, Deborah. "Namah's Womb: A Woman's Midrash of Noah's Ark." © 1989 by Deborah Kruger. Reprinted by permission of the author.

• Lanicotti, Joanne. "Huge Muscles," from *The Birth Project* by Judy Chicago. © 1985 by Judy Chicago.

• Metzger, Deena. *Tree & The Woman Who Slept with Men to Take the War Out of Them* (Oakland, Calif.: Wingbow Press, 1983).

• Monaghan, Patricia. "Burials." From *Seasons of the Witch*. Copyright © 1992 by Delphi Press, Inc. Oak Park, IL 60304. Reprinted by permission of the publisher.

• Morgan, Robin. "The Network of the Imaginary Mother," from *Upstairs in the Garden: Poems Selected and New: 1968 – 1988.* Copyright © 1990 by Robin Morgan. Reprinted by permission of the Edite Kroll Literary Agency.

• Mutén, Burleigh. "Word Magic," © 1993, "Queen Hera, 2," © 1995 and "Queen Medusa," © 1993 by Burleigh Mutén. © 1994, 1997 "Introduction" and "Epilogue."

• Noble, Vicki. Selections from pp. 38–39 and 239 of *Shakti Woman: Feeling Our Fire, Healing the World—The New Female Shamanism.* © 1991 by Vicki Noble. Reprinted by permission of HarperCollins Publishers, Inc.

• Norris, Kathleen. Excerpt from *Dakota: A Spiritual Geography.* Copyright © 1993 by Kathleen Norris. Reprinted by permission of Ticknor & Fields/Houghton Mifflin Company. All rights reserved.

• Oda, Mayumi. Excerpt from *Goddesses.* Copyright © 1981, 1988 by Mayumi Oda. First published 1981 by Lancaster-Miller Publishers. Expanded edition 1988, Volcano Press. To order, contact Volcano Press, PO Box 270 Volcano, CA 95689.

• Oda, Mayumi, trans. Excerpt from Raicho Hiratsuko, "Women's Manifesto," *Seito (Blue Stockings),* 1911.

• Orenstein, Gloria. Reprinted by permission of the publisher from *The Reflowering of the Goddess* (New York: Teachers College Press, © 1990 by Teachers College, Columbia University), p. 187. All rights reserved.

• Reis, Patricia. Excerpts from *Through the Goddess: A Woman's Way of Healing. Copyright* © 1991 by Patricia Reis. Reprinted by permission of the Crossroad Publishing Company.

• Replansky, Namoi. "Housing Shortage." © 1952. Reprinted by permission of the author.

• Rush, Anne Kent. Excerpts from *Moon, Moon.* Random House and Moon Books. Copyright © 1976 by Anne Kent Rush. Reprinted by permission of the author.

• Sarton, May. "The Invocation to Kali." Reprinted from *Selected Poems of May Sarton,* ed. Serena Sue Hilsonger and Lois Brynes, with permission of W. W. Norton & Company, Inc. Copyright © 1978 by May Sarton.

• Sarton, May. "When a woman feels alone." Reprinted from *Letters from Maine: New Poems* by May Sarton with permission of W. W. Norton & Company, Inc. Copyright © 1984 by May Sarton.

• Shange, Ntozake. "we need a god who